SELLING

to the

HEART

How most sales are really won!

SELLING

to the

HEART

How most sales are really won!

By
JACK SCHERER

Published by:
SMG Media
A division of Driving Profit LLC

Printed in the United States of America

ISBN: 978-0-9817993-3-9

TABLE OF CONTENTS

Dedication
Introduction

DEDICATION

*"**Selling to the Heart**" is dedicated to every professional salesperson who has chosen sales as one of the greatest careers in the world.*

A true professional salesperson builds trust, solves problems, builds relationships...and always sells to the heart...how most sales are really won!

INTRODUCTION

Everyone sells. The next time you go to the supermarket notice the small toddlers in the shopping cart who are trying to convince their mothers to buy a certain item that they just saw on a TV commercial. Then maybe your doorbell rings and it's a Girl Scout selling cookies and you bought them because you liked her, plus the cookies are good. Furthermore, husbands "sell" to their wives and wives "sell" to their husbands. The U.S. is the greatest country in the world and the President could be considered the greatest leader in the free world. And how did he get there? He sold his abilities to enough citizens to get the votes he needed to be elected. Everyone sells...from toddlers to the President of the U.S.

Our company has conducted many sales training seminars over the years and what we discovered is that many people have a rather negative opinion of the average salesperson. They say most salespeople are too pushy, they really do not trust them, and they seem to be too focused on making a sale versus trying to help the prospective customer.

Even though a sales career is one of the highest paid

professions in the U.S., it generally does not have a good reputation when compared to other professions. So it's up to you as a professional salesperson to separate yourself as quickly as you can from this stereotyped image of the typical salesperson. You can do this in many ways, but one of the most effective is to sell to the person's heart...build that emotional link between you and your prospects and customers and your sales will continue to grow.

In his book *"Emotional Intelligence"*, Daniel Goleman states that great leaders, entrepreneurs and sales professionals all have a high degree of emotional intelligence (E.I.)...the ability to analyze and understand other people's emotions and to adapt accordingly. The two main functions of the brain that influence our behavior—both intellectually and emotionally—are situated in different parts of our brain. The frontal cortex of the brain receives emotional input before the logical reasoning process. As a result, many people buy emotionally and then try to justify these decisions logically. This is how many of our brains are wired and why most advertising is emotionally-driven, not logically-driven.

In **Selling to the Heart,** you will learn how most sales are really won through emotional connections and triggers that are part of your sales process. In addition, this book will teach you specific techniques to become a true trusted advisor, to increase your confidence and to become a valuable problem solver, as well as many other valuable sales techniques.

Live your life from your heart, sell to the heart, and reap the many rewards that you will have throughout your life. It is almost guaranteed.

EMOTIONS WIN

*People may forget what you said, but they
will never forget how you made them feel*

In selling, many sales are won by emotional buying decisions made by your prospects. Let's use a simple example...Susan just made a large sale to Bob who is the CEO of a software company. When we asked Bob why he bought from Susan instead of from the other competitors, his response included, *"I liked her...I trusted her...she seemed to care about me...she was sincere and she seemed like a good person with whom to work."* Not once did Bob mention that she had the best product knowledge or even the lowest price. Bob bought emotionally from Susan. Bob bought from his heart.

In sales, there are two concepts that are called "soft knowledge" and "hard knowledge." Soft knowledge is the person, their character, their body language, their style, the distinct impression that they give. On the other hand, there is the hard knowledge that the salesperson has called product knowledge. In most sales processes, the soft knowledge always precedes the hard knowledge. As someone once said, *"they want to know how much you care, before they care how much you know."*

In the case of Susan and her competition, as in many sales situations, Bob bought from Susan emotionally. Make no mistake, product knowledge is extremely important, but in most cases the softer side of the salesperson will be the dominant factor in making the sale. Emotions often dominate reason in life as well as in sales. Your prospects don't really buy your services or products…they buy how they *perceive* using them will make them feel.

In reality, we all have two different minds…emotional and rational. This dichotomy can be called heart and head. The more intense the feeling about something the more dominant the emotional mind becomes and the less effective the rational mind. Did you ever think and analyze that the billions of dollars spent on national advertising are designed to trigger our emotions to buy a specific product or service, not our logical reasoning?

The emotional mind is much quicker than the rational mind in making instant decisions without any type of rational discernment. Emotions create either a good impression or a bad impression of a person. Emotions create what people often call a "gut feeling" about them. In other words, based upon past situations, the emotional drivers stored in the subconscious mind will cause a person to make an intuitive judgment about that specific decision. Logic and rational thinking appears secondary in many cases.

In a survey of 10,000 people who were asked why they buy from salespeople, their responses included:

- Confidence
- Quality
- Service
- Selection
- Price

As you can see, the confidence that you instill in your prospects represents the number one reason why they will buy from you.

One of the best books ever written about sales is *How To Win Friends and Influence People* by Dale Carnegie. Although published in 1937, this book is still considered to be the bible of human interaction. In the book, Mr. Carnegie discusses specific principles for life and, as a salesperson, how to enjoy the success that you need and deserve. These principles, as described by Dale Carnegie, are practical and emotionally-driven...

- **Compliment:** give people sincere compliments about themselves

- **Appreciation**: show people appreciation…the two most important words in the English language are "thank you"
- **Interest**: show genuine interest in the other person…they really like to know that you care about them
- **Smile**: a smile is the greatest form of non-verbal communication that we have
- **Name**: use the person's name because using a person's name is one of the best things that we all like to hear
- **Acknowledgment**: give sincere recognition for a person's and their company's accomplishments
- **Yes**: concentrate on getting your prospect to agree with you and say "yes" as many times as they possibly can
- **Listen**: strive to get the person to talk as much as possible rather than you dominating the conversation
- **Empathy**: communicate real feelings and understanding from the person's point of view
- **Humility**: show an element of humility…no one is good at everything
- **Permission**: instead of commanding or controlling the interaction, ask permission to do something for them

- **Optimistic:** be happy and talk in a positive manner...eliminate all negative thinking and phrases from your conversation

As you can see, selling emotionally is a major key in achieving the sales success you desire. Using these emotional triggers will help you with developing trust and confidence for you and your company. The result will be new customers, repeat sales, and a greater sense of personal achievement.

Chapter
2

YOU ARE THE BRAND

Your personal brand influences many sales

Most people buy proven brands. As a sales professional, you are the brand. In addition, your company is also the brand…and in most cases a person is buying you first and your company second. Prospects do not buy because of how good you are at what you do…they really buy because of how good you are at *who you are.*

If a prospect does not trust you and you do not project an honest image, they will probably not have a good image of your company either. Someone once said, *"image is everything."* While that might be a little too "Madison Avenue," as professional salespeople we have an obligation to generate a good image quickly.

If you create a poor image initially, the prospect will shut down and try to end your sales presentation as quickly as possible because they have already decided they do not want to do business with you. Of course, the opposite is true. If you create a good impression initially, the prospect will be more likely to listen to you and consider buying from you. In other words, prospects hear what they see…they trust their eyes before they trust their ears.

How do you create a good first impression when making a sales call? There are two major components of creating a good image: appearance and body language.

Not everyone has the looks of a Hollywood movie star but that is not necessary. In making sales you don't have to look like a movie star but you have to project and convey a professional image in your appearance. Here are some good tips for creating a professional image as a sales leader.

- Wear a jacket when meeting a client or prospect
- Carry a high quality leather briefcase or portfolio to your meeting
- The power colors in business are dark neutral colors like black, charcoal, gray, navy, and dark brown. These traditional business colors communicate professionalism and competence. A sales professional always has his or her traditional suit jacket, dress, slacks, and skirts in these dark neutral tones
- The second element in creating a good image is your body language. Psychologists tell us that up to 80% of what we communicate is really through our body language.
- As professional salespeople we should also be able to read a person's body language to decide how the prospect is responding to our presentation.

What makes you and your company strong is not initially the products or services but the image that you project in the customer's mind, because we all buy from a state of mind. In order to get the best positioning in the customer's mind you need to project the image of being a specialist or a subject matter expert. The business world is very competitive and your prospects will buy more from a specialist than from someone who appears to be all things to all people. If you position yourself as a subject matter expert in the prospect's mind, you are more likely to win the sale. The application of your knowledge is the power to solve a person's problem, often leading to a sale.

As a sales professional building your personal brand, you will need to be a specialist in three key areas. First, you need to become a specialist in your company's products and services. The most important point here is that you need to communicate the benefits, not features, of what you are selling and how they will help the prospect solve their problems. Do not make the mistake of "information dumping"…thinking that the more information you give, the better your presentation will be. Your prospect will get bored and really stop listening to you. Information overload is not effective in selling…it's really boring.

The second key area in building your personal brand as a specialist is to be an expert in the industry in which you are selling. For example, if you are selling specialized software solutions to the legal industry, become knowledgeable about certain aspects of the legal industry. When you are meeting with an attorney you can have an intelligent conversation about their business, representing a better position in the prospect's mind for you as a professional and a trusted advisor. You will be viewed as an industry specialist and not just a salesperson.

Another method of building your personal brand is to know about your major competitors and most importantly, why your company is better. The key here is not to criticize your competitors and to acknowledge that they are good companies but be able to explain why your company is better. Again, you will be viewed as a specialist in your industry and will be helping position yourself as the best in that industry.

In order to take the edge off of your sales calls you need to develop rapport with your prospect. The better rapport you create with your prospect the better your communication will be in creating an element of persuasion. Good rapport helps to build your personal brand.

There are a number of proven ways you can create rapport with your prospect in order to develop your own personal brand. First, you need the prospect to feel comfortable and eliminate the feeling that you are just there to try to sell them something. Unfortunately, in many sales situations, the atmosphere can be adversarial—you against them—not a good way to sell.

You can make your prospect feel comfortable in a number of ways. You should be relaxed, confident, and conversational. Good sales presentations are conversational and not a lecture. If you appear to be relaxed, your prospect will also become relaxed and the quality of your communication will increase and develop into a better relationship with your prospect.

Dale Carnegie said that you can create more friends in two weeks by getting them to talk about themselves, than you can in two years talking about yourself. The key here is to get them to talk about themselves and not talk about you. You can do this by asking good, open-ended questions such as…How did you get into this business? What are your business goals, etc. When you show sincere interest in the other person and really listen to them, they will like you. If they like you, you are in the process of building your personal brand, which will enhance your chances of winning new sales.

Another way to create rapport with your prospect is to create a bond—something that you both have in common. Again, to find this common bond you have to ask questions. For example, you may ask where they grew up, went to college, etc. Or if you are in someone's office and you notice they have golf pictures on the wall, you may ask where they play golf or if they played in any tournaments recently? If someone really likes golf and they are good at it, they will love to talk about it and then if you play golf too you can share your experiences. You have just created a bond with your prospect...chemistry is created.

Building your personal brand is an ongoing experience that you can improve on a consistent basis because people buy from people they like and it's up to you to build a strong personal brand...and people buy brands.

Chapter
3

TRUSTED ADVISOR

*As a sales professional your most important
asset is trust*

Since building trust is one of the most important parts of actually getting a sale, let us analyze how it's done and how you might not achieve it.

Many sales are lost because the salesperson does not create a relationship and does not solve a problem or create a sense of trust in their company or themselves. They are viewed as just an ordinary salesperson trying to sell something.

Unfortunately, trust has been fading in recent times in our country—in politics, in business, perhaps in some families and marriages—where trust should be the cornerstone of lasting relationships. But trust isn't about business or politics or marriages, it's about life. If trust is the cornerstone of your life, you will create friendships, business relationships, and ultimately achieve your life's goals because you are a person who inspires trust from others.

The **best way** to create trust as a salesperson is to focus on these major elements: Credibility, Caring, Character, and Commitment:

CREDIBILITY

- Be an expert in your niched field and in your industry; know what's going on and be able to talk intelligently about the products and services you are representing and how they will benefit your prospect
- Don't act like a salesperson—be a problem solver, working with the prospect as a partner/team to help their business grow
- Make sure the statements you make are always accurate, and avoid broad general statements, such as "we are the best and fastest growing company in town"
- Speak in facts that you can prove, not opinions
- Never, never exaggerate
- Use references and testimonials—have these available to show during your presentation

CARING

- Listen to your prospect; show a real interest in their needs; they want to know how much you care before they care how much you know
- About 65% of all buying decisions are emotionally made so sell to the heart first and the head second

- Listen more than you talk
- Ask good open-ended questions and then repeat the answers to be sure you understand what they are saying
- Note how the prospect feels while answering and try to get them to expand on things they are excited about
- Provide possible solutions for them…people like to be helped

CHARACTER

- Radiate integrity; how you do anything is how you do everything so show that you can be trusted to tell the truth and always put the prospect's best interests first
- Experts say that about 80% of what we communicate is really through our body language so be sure to present yourself well
- Look professional
- Be punctual
- Make good eye contact
- Have a firm handshake
- Be calm, confident & conversational
- Never cross your arms or put your hand over your mouth while talking
- Create a comfortable environment where the prospect wants to buy from you
- Salespeople have a certain disadvantage caused by

the general misconception that salespeople will do or say anything to get a sale. You need to overcome that misconception to be able to partner with your prospect

COMMITMENT

- Do what you say you are going to do, and deliver it when you say will; don't make excuses
- Go the extra mile to create that all-important competitive edge that makes you and your company truly unique

To excel in your sales career, it is important that your prospects view you as a trusted advisor versus just the ordinary salesperson who is perceived as trying to make a quick sale.

Sales professionals who are perceived as trusted advisors have the following skill sets and they think long term:

- They are experts in their position and in their industry
- They don't sell but they create opportunities where the prospect wants to buy; they solve problems; they bring new ideas to old problems; they have the attitude of helping versus selling; they are perceived as a valuable resource to help the prospect really grow their business

On the other hand, the average salesperson has these characteristics:

- They think short term
- They think sell, sell, sell and close, close, close
- They struggle to maintain a positive image in the prospect's mind
- They "information dump" thinking that the prospects are buying features and not customized solutions
- They do not create or maintain relationships
- They create pressure on themselves to sell more rather than trying to help their prospect achieve success
- They are self-focused versus customer-focused

Strive to be a trusted advisor, not just a salesperson, and your sales will soar!

Chapter

4

POSITIVE ATTITUDE

Believe it and you can achieve it

Let's say there is a company that will be making a large purchase and they are interviewing three competing companies to see which company can offer the best value, but not necessarily the lowest price.

So salesperson "A" visits the company and makes a presentation to the three partners. This person seems knowledgeable about their company but makes negative comments about their competitors. In addition, the salesperson lacks positive energy and does not project an attitude of helping or consulting in order to solve problems for the prospect. This person is perceived as somewhat negative, although well-versed in product knowledge.

The next salesperson "B" makes a call on the same three partners. This person projects an element of confidence but again is perceived as somewhat indifferent to the needs of the prospect. In fact, this person appears to be just going through the motions to get the sale.

And finally, the third salesperson "C" makes a sales call on the prospects. When this person walks into the room to meet the decision makers, she lights up the room by radiating a very strong positive attitude about herself and about her company. Most importantly, she displays a strong positive attitude about helping the prospect. She listens very well, does not criticize the competition, and presents herself as a true trusted advisor versus just a salesperson. In addition, good product knowledge is displayed.

It is very clear that salesperson "C" has the best chance of winning the sale primarily because of the strong positive attitude that she projected. She had true passion for her role as a salesperson who was full of energy and projected an attitude of caring about the prospect and helping them solve specific problems.

In his book, *Think and Grow Rich,* Napoleon Hill discusses in each of the chapters, a plan for success in life and in business. Much of his advice is based upon some of the greatest business successes of all time, including Andrew Carnegie, Henry Ford, Thomas Edison, FDR, to name just a few. In order to be an outstanding sales professional, you need to be mentally success-driven. Here are some great quotes that summarize the attainment of success:

- *"If you think you can, you are right; if you think you can't, you are right"*
- *"Believe it and you can achieve it"*
- *"The majority of people meet with failure because they lack persistence in creating new plans to take advantage of the plans which failed"*
- *"Set a goal and a deadline for its attainment"*
- *"No one ever achieved worthwhile success without first finding themselves with at least one foot hanging over the brink of failure"*

Unfortunately, our educational systems from kindergarten through college devote little time to the power of positive thinking—one of the key cards in your deck. It is the fuel that will fight adversities...the fuel that will help you reach your dreams...and the key to your success in both your life and in business.

In one of his books Napoleon Hill speaks about building blocks that help you to achieve your goals. It is not a question of your race, gender, education or where you were born. It is a question of how you mentally program your thinking—something that is your choice and no one else's. If you believe your sales career will be successful, execute well, and never quit, you will reach or exceed your sales goals.

Self-talk is a thinking process that you do each second of every day and you have the chance to produce self-talk that is positive or self-talk that is negative. Surveys that have been conducted over the years found that the average person has over 5,000 self-talks or thoughts per day. The amazing fact is that most of the self-talk is negative. According to research the average person's mind is programmed in a very negative, rather than a very positive, manner. Herein lies the problem of our success or lack of success. Positive self-talk and continuous self-affirmation conditions the mind for success just like lifting weights helps build muscles in your body for additional strength.

Another aspect of self-talk is that it creates the power of visualization, whereby you program your mind and your thinking about the outcome before it actually happens. In other words, you visualize in your mind what you want to achieve and how it will happen—the outcome—before it actually happens. You have to really believe that you can be successful in your sales career before it will happen. Remember, *believe it and you can achieve it.*

One of the best methods of creating power of belief in yourself and your sales career is to completely eliminate any of the following thoughts from your daily self-talks:

- *"I think I might get fired"*

- *"I probably will not reach my quota"*
- *"My boss does not like me"*
- *"I need to get with a better company"*
- *"I wish we had better prices and products"*
- *"My sales territory is bad"*

These are all negative thoughts that will hinder your belief that you will be successful. They are like anchors around your neck pulling you into the ocean where you could drown.

Another key to establishing a strong belief in yourself and your sales career is to focus each day on what you have instead of what you don't have. No one has everything. My mother gave us good advice a long time ago when she said, *"count your blessings"* and she was certainly correct! It is quite easy to build a case against ourselves when things don't go as expected, such as missing your monthly sales goals three months in a row, but that only creates what we call downward spiraling. It's important to believe in yourself and focus on the strengths and abilities that God has given you and use these effectively in the execution of winning new sales. Someone once said, *"A wise man will be a master of his own mind; a weak man will be a slave to it."*

We all have habits – some good, some bad. In fact, studies indicate that about 90% of what we do each day is based upon habit. You can eliminate bad habits by focusing on some good habits that you have developed over the years to be successful.

Here are some key habits you need to acquire and use to be successful in your sales career:

- **Strong Sense of Purpose**—this is the starting point of your success. You must clearly develop the habit of setting and reaching goals and sticking to this plan. Eliminate the habit of making excuses about why you cannot reach your predetermined goals. Anything is yours if you are willing to pay the price.

- **Tenacity**—having the habit of tenacity is the power to keep moving forward through all barriers and roadblocks. Perseverance will often be the key element between success and failure. Winston Churchill was known for having said, *"Never, never, never quit."* Vince Lombardi, the great coach of the Green Bay Packers, once said, *"Our greatest glory was not in never failing, but rising after we failed."*

- **Self-discipline**—a habit that can be defined as doing something you do not want to do. All great achievers in business, the arts, and sports practice self-discipline. One of the reasons that there is such a high failure rate in sales is that the majority of salespeople are not disciplined enough to prospect for new business because of all the adversity that comes from cold calling. They do not like rejection and many salespeople just mentally quit.

- **Faith**—develop great faith in yourself and most importantly, in God, that he will help you along the way in your quest for success. Remember, there is nothing that you and God cannot do together.

Your actions are always controlled by your thoughts. In life and in business you do not get what you want or what you need, you really get what you expect. Life is a self-fulfilling prophecy based upon your thoughts which, ultimately, should create the right actions. Compelling actions are always jumpstarted by a burning desire to reach certain goals. If you have a burning desire which will fuel actions, combined with good abilities, your sales career will be a success.

In his book, *The 7 Habits of Highly Effective People,* Stephen Covey says to always begin with the end in sight. In other words, what results do you want from your actions? Successful people develop the habit of visualization—the mental power to visualize the result they want to achieve even before they start.

In our sales training classes and seminars we ask managers what they want their sales team to achieve from our programs. At the top of the list is teaching salespeople how to close more sales. In other words, they want more results. What is interesting about this is that sales results will occur if the salesperson presents their services or products correctly in a consistent manner. In most cases, the prospect will then close himself and often say, *"what is the next step?"*

So results are largely dependent upon proper preparation and the previously discussed steps...self-talk, belief, habits, and actions. Focus on these and you will obtain the results you want in your sales career and also in your life.

Positive thinking is a function of the mind—we are what we think and believe—the results usually follow in a positive manner. When we radically change our thoughts, we can radically change our outcomes.

THOUGHTS
"Keep your thoughts positive because your thoughts become your words"

WORDS
"Keep your words positive because your words become your behavior"

BEHAVIOR

"Keep your behavior positive because your behavior becomes your habits"

HABITS

"Keep your habits positive because your habits become your values"

VALUES

"Keep your values positive because your values become your destiny"

In order to develop a more positive attitude about yourself, your life, and your career think of your mind as a garden. A garden can grow weeds or flowers. Weeds will grow if you do not cultivate the soil and remove small weeds as they occur so they don't spread. On the other hand you can plant flowers in your mind if you take care of the soil, provide sufficient watering of the flowers, proper nourishment and then watch them bloom. Always plant flowers in your mind and get rid of the weeds and you will have a garden flourishing with positive attitude to help your sales blossom into full growth.

Chapter 5

LISTEN

Top performing salespeople have mastered the art of listening

The better you listen to your prospects, the more likely you are perceived to be a good salesperson by the prospect. By listening efficiently you present the image that you care and you are there to try to solve problems…not there to try to *sell them something*. There is an emotional and trusted connection that you will project to create a bond with your prospect.

A salesperson we spoke with had recently won a major sale so we asked why he thought he won the sale and he said that he asked his client the same question, and the client simply said, "you listened better."

In many surveys it was found that the majority of prospects and business decision-makers think that many salespeople talk far too much and do not listen very well. In fact, in most sales presentations the salesperson will "information dump," thinking that the more information they can give, the better chance of winning the sale. The opposite is actually true. The salesperson who asks the right open-ended questions and then concentrates on listening to the prospect's answers, has a much greater chance of winning the sale by satisfying specific needs and wants. The word "listen" and the word "silent" have the same letters.

In Stephen Covey's best-selling book, *The Seven Habits of Highly Effective People,* he says that most people are not good listeners. He says the major reason for this is that most people listen with the intent to reply and not to try to understand. Many salespeople are preparing what they are going to say next or questions they are going to ask or topics they want to talk about, rather than really focusing on what the prospect is saying. When you think about what you are going to say next, you are not actively listening. In sales this is crucial because the prospect may be disclosing what needs they have and the salesperson may not be listening to the clues they are giving which would help to win the sale.

Another reason that many people are not good at listening is that the average person speaks at about 150 words per minute but has the capacity to listen at the rate of 500 words per minute. So our ratio of listening far exceeds the person's ability to speak and therefore our minds wander, resulting in not completely listening to the person speaking.

In the optimal sales presentation, the salesperson should listen 65% of the time and speak only 35% of the time. This is true based upon the following cliché...*the questions are really the answers.* In other words, professional, high-achieving salespeople ask good open-ended questions and then let the prospect speak, listening carefully to find potential needs and possible solutions to help solve their problems. Every sale is really a solution to a problem, but we need to be very proactive listeners to help solve the prospect's problems.

Listening is a difficult skill to master but there are a number of ways you can improve and become a better listener, which will increase your sales:

- **Concentrate** – really focus on what the prospect is saying. Shut off all the thoughts in your head, specifically those about what you are going to say next. Pay attention and focus on certain words and how the prospect emphasizes specific words and how they might repeat these words, which indicates what is important to the prospect...what their "hot buttons" may be.
- **Acknowledge** –acknowledge and make comments about what your prospect says. This accomplishes two things: it shows your prospect that you are really listening and that you care about their thoughts and needs. If you acknowledge an idea that the prospect

has, it may spark another idea that they want to talk about. It has been proven that top-performing salespeople acknowledge a prospect's comments twice as often as a mediocre salesperson does.

- **Summarize** – after the prospect has spoken about their concerns, their needs, and objections, summarize the thoughts at the end of the conversation. That way both you and your prospect can understand the big picture and what they may really need.
- **Do not interrupt** – this shows a lack of respect for your prospect that what they want to say is less important than what you want to say. Give them the opportunity to speak without any real interruptions from you.

And, finally, to project that you are really listening to your prospect you must show good body language, which includes...

- **Eye contact** – have your eyes focused on your prospect. This indicates that you are sincere and truly interested in what they are saying.
- **Leaning forward** – when you lean forward it shows you are truly engaged in what your prospect is saying.
- **Smiling** – a smile says that you like the prospect and shows that you are in agreement with him.

- **Nodding your head** – also a very effective, nonverbal communication technique that communicates that you are really listening and you are agreeing with what she is saying.

Remember, about 80% of what we communicate is really through nonverbal means of communication. Always remember that the top sales professionals in any industry have mastered the skill of active listening to generate more sales.

Chapter
6

CARING

*They want to know how much you care before they
care how much you know*

Most prospects want to know how much you care before
they care how much you know. Let's use the following
example. Bill calls on a prospect and projects the
impression that he is there to make a sale. He has
excellent product knowledge but seems to be cold and
somewhat indifferent to the prospect's business. In other
words, no sense of caring is projected to the prospect—in
either verbal or nonverbal communication. Instead, the
salesperson focuses on the depth of knowledge that he has
and all of the features and benefits of his company and
tries to close the sale.

Next Tom, from another company, makes a call on the
same prospect. He immediately shows a keen interest in
the prospect and how he feels he can help them—versus
just trying to sell them something. In other words, Tom
demonstrates a strong sense of caring about the prospect's
needs. In the same sense, he has good knowledge about
the company and projects a strong sense of emotional
bonding with the prospect. The emotional connection was

made between the salesperson and the prospect. It's quite obvious that Tom has a much greater chance of winning the sale because he seems to really care about helping the prospect. When you, as a salesperson, have the best interest of your prospect at heart, you know it is leading to a greater chance of winning a new sale.

Another way to show that you care about your prospect is to be curious. Ask good questions to learn more about the business. Your natural curiosity will show them that you have empathy...that you care about them. Reverse the rules...put yourself in the prospect's shoes. If you were them, what would you want to hear? Then present from that standpoint...not what you want to say to sell them something, but what you think your prospect really wants and needs to hear.

Connect on a human level by showing a caring attitude toward your prospect – as a helpful, trusted advisor, not just as a salesperson. You must remember that the key to most sales is to connect emotionally with your prospect. They end up buying versus you just selling. By caring you are really selling to their heart...how most sales are really won.

Chapter
7

BELIEVE

To reach your sales goals you must not only act,
but also believe

When you show an attitude of believing in yourself and your company, you will be more persuasive in your sales presentations. Belief is the starting point of all great accomplishments, including winning a new customer. Belief in your own success is one basic essential all successful salespeople have. Believe it and you can achieve it.

A strong belief in your selling ability will equal better results and winning more new clients. This occurs in various stages. Strong belief equates to a stronger desire and creates continuous action which then develops good results and continuous new sales. Your motivation increases when you actually believe you can reach a specific goal, but your mind must always be in the belief mode.

To increase the power of your belief, you must focus on these four key elements:

- *Belief in yourself*
- *Belief in your company*
- *Belief in your persistence*
- *Belief that you can reach your goals*

The starting point of your belief system is you. To really believe in yourself you must concentrate on the positive aspects of who you are. You must then think in a positive manner to condition your mind as a *positive thought factory*. Think about what you have versus what you do not have. Belief in yourself is the real gauge that regulates what you accomplish in your sales career and in life.

Unfortunately, the majority of people's minds are programmed in a negative manner. As we indicated, about 80% of a person's thinking is negative versus positive. Just think, if 80% of your thoughts were positive, how your belief in yourself would increase. The key is to condition your mind in the positive belief that you can become a high-performing salesperson.

The second aspect of increasing your belief system is to really believe in your company, its products and services. We all sell in a very competitive world that is getting more competitive each year. No one company is perfect or has the perfect selection of products or services. The key here is to focus on the positive attributes of your company and not any of its shortcomings. When you believe in your company, your energy will increase when presenting the value of your company's products and services. Your belief will show conviction, which will increase the quality of your presentation, resulting in more sales.

Many salespeople are not successful because they just recite words without any conviction and the prospect can quickly see their lack of belief, which then affects their decision to purchase from them or not. On the other hand, if you sell with a strong amount of conviction combined with a high level of passion, your closing ratios will accelerate at a higher rate.

You must also believe that you have the necessary persistence to overcome all the adversity that comes with a career in sales. The average salesperson hears more no's than yeses so it's very easy to become discouraged when selling. It's much easier to quit when you get rejected so many times. However, it takes a strong amount of courage to keep moving on and still having a positive attitude to succeed. Persistence can be defined as a strong inner strength which stays with you in overcoming obstacles. Persistence is not given to you but is something you have to earn. It's one of the most necessary components you must have to become an exceptional sales leader. It's a refusal to quit regardless of the circumstances. It's a spark plug that will ignite your ability to achieve and become a very successful sales professional.

The fourth element of belief is your ability to believe that you can achieve your goals. A goal is an objective…it's a purpose that you can achieve if you believe you can. A wish on the other hand, is a thought or something that you would like to achieve but it is merely a dream without much conviction or passion.

When you believe in yourself and your company, your mental toughness will help you become a high-performance sales professional. If this strong belief hits the heart of your prospect, your sales will continue to increase.

Chapter
8

STORIES
Good stories always touch the heart

Let's think about the following scenario. You are calling on a new prospect to win a new account. You can lead with telling successful stories about how you have helped similar businesses achieve more sales through the use of your company's products and services. The other choices are to "information dump"—talking about the various features of your company services or products. Which tactic has the most success? The answer, of course, is telling success stories that your prospect can relate to. In most cases, if you overwhelm the prospect with information they will lose attention during your presentation and not really focus on what you are presenting. You become a boring salesperson.

Stories sell because in most cases they are emotionally-driven. Reciting information that is perceived as boring and maybe not even relevant to them doesn't work. Unfortunately, there are many salespeople who try to sell through "information overload" versus telling relevant success stories that truly touch the prospect's heart and head.

All great salespeople tell success stories from their past sales achievements. It's human nature to like to listen to stories rather than some type of sales lecture. We probably got hooked on stories when we were just small children and our parents read to us from books which were filled with humor and drama and a sense of excitement. We listen with our hearts and we remember emotional things which are embedded in our brains forever.

Stories and phrases filled with emotion have a great impact on many people in a planned direction. Let us use some examples...

- President John F. Kennedy's famous line from his inaugural speech, "Ask not what your country can do for you, ask what you can do for your country"
- Rev. Martin Luther King, Jr.'s famous "I Have A Dream" speech that really moved people to a higher level of passion and belief in themselves and our great country with its many opportunities

They both spoke with a high degree of emotion. The next time you are at church, pay attention to the reaction of the people in the church when the speaker/minister/priest tells a story about a specific family or incident. You will find that all eyes and ears are locked onto the story and most significantly, that they relate to the story and remember it long afterwards. Stories are emotionally-driven to command attention whether during a church service, a political campaign, or a sales call.

A suggestion for you as a professional salesperson would be to have a selection of stories you can tell your prospect that describe some of your past sales successes. You will find that this is quite effective and the persuasion factor will increase. There are basically three types of stories you can tell as a sales professional that can resonate with your prospects:

- **Problem Solving Story**—tell a story about how your company's products or services solved a real problem for your customer and what they gained.
- **Similar Customer Story**—tell a story about a customer with a business similar to your prospect's...that they can quickly relate to and see how you helped the other customer and may therefore be able to do the same or a similar thing for their company.
- **Going the Extra Mile Story**—tell a story about how you went the "extra mile" to help a customer. This will demonstrate that you are a unique and helpful sales professional with whom your prospect should want to do business.

In summary, becoming a good storyteller will increase your persuasion of your prospect for the following reasons:

- People remember short stories before they remember facts and data

- Most stories are associated with entertainment and people like to be entertained

- Stories activate previous experiences which create credibility in what you are presenting

- Stories create a cause and effect scenario helping the decision making process by a prospect

- Stories go to the frontal cortex of the brain where we experience our emotions leading to our actions

Become a good storyteller and you will become a better salesperson.

Chapter
9

THE EXTRA MILE

There is never a traffic jam at the extra mile

If you want to be an exceptional salesperson you need to go the "extra mile" for your prospects. Someone once said, *"There's never a traffic jam at the extra mile."*

Going the extra mile is a habit that you need to develop so that it becomes part of your turnkey selling process. As you develop the habit of going the extra mile for your prospects and customers, you will distinguish yourself as being different and more professional than most of your competitors. The *"Law of Increasing Returns"* states that, "the more you give, the more you get." High performers go the extra mile by doing things that are not expected of them; in fact, they *under-promise and over-deliver*. If you show real concern for each prospect and customer and do the things that go beyond the scope of duty, your sales will begin to increase. Do not expect immediate results...but the results will come to you.

Nordstrom's Department Store, which was started in Seattle in the 1920s, has established a consistent reputation for going the extra mile in serving its customers. Their management and, most importantly, their sales associates practice superior customer service on a daily basis, which in turn drives customer loyalty for repeat sales. In one case a customer turned in a tire to Nordstrom's and was given a refund for the tire... Nordstrom's does not even sell tires...but they went that extra mile for their customer!

Here's another example of how a person went the extra mile and was rewarded. A new college graduate applied for a sales position with a company. The interview went quite well and at the end of the interview she was told that her education was good but she didn't have enough sales experience to be offered the position so she should call them back in a few years. After the interview she went to the closest florist and bought a small green plant and brought it back to the company. She left it with the receptionist at the front desk with a handwritten note for the person who had interviewed her that said *"I know I might be too green for the job but if you give me the opportunity to sell for your company, I promise I will exceed your expectations."* The next day she was offered a sales position. She went the extra mile and she won!

By going the extra mile you develop a positive and pleasing personality which your prospects and customers will appreciate. As we discussed, many buying decisions are emotionally based and your attitude of going the extra mile can lead to new and repeat sales.

As a sales professional, here are some practical ways you can go that extra mile for your prospects and your customers...

- **Thank you notes** – send a personal handwritten thank you note after each sale...*business goes where it's invited and stays where it's appreciated*
- **Always be giving** – there are many ways you can give...lunches...emailing articles...sending copies of articles in magazines with information the prospect/customer may be interested in but perhaps did not see, etc.
- **Referrals** – become a source of referrals for your customers and your prospects
- **Industry expert** – study your industry and provide helpful information to your clients...good salespeople are always valuable sources of information

By going the extra mile, you will eventually win the race and receive the sales rewards of new customers, referrals, and increased commissions. By going the extra mile you make yourself truly unique in the crowded marketplace.

Chapter
10

ADVERSITY

It's not about how many times you get hit; it's about how many times you get back up that really counts

How you deal with adversities is one of the key elements of life…and a great indicator of your future sales success. To be emotionally strong you need to overcome the many rejections that occur in your selling efforts. When you study successful salespeople it is their ability to overcome adversity that really makes them successful.

Let us use an example of how adversity and worry could affect your sales performance. Then we'll discuss what you can do about it. Tom is used to achieving his sales goals and has been in the top 20% of his company for three consecutive years. The new year started not long ago but Tom did not make a single sale for two months. He encountered setback after setback and continuous rejection of his presentations. This adversity truly affected Tom's motivation and confidence in himself. The adversity that he encountered turned into a constant source of worry…worry that he had lost his sales touch; worry that he might even lose his job despite the strong reputation that he had earned over the years.

Maybe you can relate to Tom's situation because you have encountered or maybe are currently encountering the horrible feeling of worry caused by continuous adversity in your sales career or even in your personal life.

Well, there's good news for you because there are proven methods to eliminate most of your worries. Worry can be described as a negative self-induced thought pattern that is manufactured by a person in their head. By repeating these negative thoughts, worry becomes a habit which is difficult to break unless positive actions are taken.

One of the most effective ways to conquer worry and adversity is to replace those negative thoughts with continuous positive thoughts. There are two great statistics that prove this principle to be effective. First principle: states that 95% of what we do is based upon the habits we create for ourselves. If negative thoughts lead to the habit of creating and repeating negative thoughts, then thinking positive thoughts and repeating them will create a positive method of thinking that will block out many of the petty worries that enter into your mind. In other words, fill your mind with positive thoughts on a continuous basis and you will develop the habit of positive thinking which is directly opposed to negative thinking.

The second principle that you should understand is that studies show that 92% of a person's worries are self-generated and will never happen. They are "mental monsters" that a person has developed through repetition of negative thoughts turned into habits...and the only person in control of these habits is you.

Another method of conquering worry is to pick your worries apart and analyze each part of the worry. Many elements of a large worry problem are composed of multiple small worries that can be analyzed and eliminated. By studying the small components, you can define the problem and develop possible solutions to defeat the monumental worry in a clear and rational manner.

To become a strong, emotionally-driven sales professional you will encounter adversity—it's just part of the sales game. Adversity is inevitable so we can all accept it as a normal occurrence and move on. The key here is to hit adversity and worry right in the face. Rise above these elements and you will become stronger and stronger as a sales leader in your profession. It's not how many times you get hit...it's how many times you get back up that really counts.

In conclusion, here is a brief story about a salesperson that I know pretty well...

This person bought an advertising franchise and moved from another city to begin his new career in Atlanta. He was really excited about this new opportunity because since college, he wanted to own his own business. In this new position, he made presentations to companies about how they could increase their sales through his new advertising program. The business was more difficult than it seemed. In one particular week, the salesperson made over fifty cold calls each day, Monday to Friday without getting one single sale. Toward the end of the week, the salesperson doubted the value of the franchise that he bought and doubted his ability to sell. On Friday, it started to rain in the afternoon but the salesperson was still making calls door to door because he was determined to get a sale for that week. About 4:30 p.m., in the pouring down rain, he made another call on a business trying to maintain a positive attitude in his presentation. The prospect said "yes," he would buy his program.

This salesperson failed to quit and his efforts were finally rewarded after receiving over 200 "no's" that week. More importantly, that one sale was a turning point in this person's sales career. He ended up owning the #2 franchise in the United States, was elected president of the franchise association and helped train other franchisees in their sales techniques. I asked this salesperson what kept him going when he could have quit Thursday and taken off Friday as a day of rest. He said he needed a sale to erase the rejection he received that particular week. He also mentioned one statement that he learned a long time ago, *"A winner never quits, a quitter never wins."* This salesperson's experience helped him achieve more confidence in his ability to overcome adversity. It was a turning point in his sales career as he also became the top salesperson nationwide in the franchise group and won five national sales awards.

Adversity is a part of selling. Learn how to overcome it and you will become a sales leader.

Chapter

11

PROBLEM SOLVING

Most sales are really solutions to problems

When you make a sales call on a prospect, they do not want to be sold something...they want their problems solved.

By being perceived as a problem solver by the prospect versus a salesperson, you can connect with the prospect better. You need to position yourself as a valuable member of their team and a consultant who solves their problems. You become a provider of key solutions to your prospect's problems. In order for you to become this problem solver you need to ask probing, open-ended questions about your prospect's business. You must create a bridge between a prospect's business and your company's customized solutions. When you create this bridge in the prospect's mind you become a member of their team...you become a solution.

Salespeople can be divided into three groups: those who sell products and services, those who sell just the best price, and those who sell solutions. The solution salesperson will be in the top echelon of any company and will always be in demand—the top 5-10% of any sales team.

The following is a profile of an **Average Salesperson** who sells products or services or the lowest price but does not lead with any problem solving techniques:

- Does not have a pre-call plan
- Does not ask enough questions (or the wrong questions) to uncover prospect's real needs or problems
- Fails to show real concern for helping the prospect—is just trying to sell them something
- Information dumps instead of building the bridge to solve the prospect's problems
- Does not have any type of commitment when he leaves the appointment
- Generally acts like a professional "visitor"—not a true problem solving expert
- Has a tendency to over-promise and under-deliver
- Does not follow up very well—maybe just once or twice
- Acts like a "salesperson" rather than a true "sales consultant" and problem solver
- Generally believes that the lowest price wins the sale

On the other hand, **Top Salespeople**, according to a study of 500 sales calls made in 24 different industries, do the following:

- They get the prospect involved in the conversation early, late, and often
- They uncover the prospect's needs before mentioning a product or service
- They acknowledge and support the prospect's comments twice as often as mediocre performers. They also asked 25% more open-ended questions, looking for solutions to problems
- They turnaround the prospect's negative attitudes; remembering that successful sales calls contain almost 50% more objections than unsuccessful calls

According to various studies, the majority of businesses want a solution-driven salesperson and not just a salesperson trying to earn higher commissions. Salespeople just by the nature of their profession have the cards stacked against them...until they prove that they offer real solutions to a prospect's problems.

A solution-driven salesperson can be an invaluable asset by providing helpful consultation to the prospect. Like a doctor or attorney, the salesperson is in the position of consulting and providing solutions...and making money in the process. The key here is to connect emotionally as quickly as you can with the prospect so you are perceived as a true problem solver...not just another salesperson.

Chapter
12

RELATIONSHIPS
Build good relationships and the repeat sales will follow

The key to long-term growth for any business is repeat customers...and the key to repeat customers is to build good relationships. In 1937, Dale Carnegie said that if you embark on a sales career, try to make sure that you get into a business where you can establish a relationship in order to generate new sales and also repeat customers. Building relationships is about feelings. Winning in sales is about these feelings and the relationships that you create.

As we discussed, many buying decisions are made emotionally. As effective salespeople we must create relationships built on trust and service to foster repeat sales. Here's a summary of what customers like and dislike about relationships with salespeople as reported by a number of surveys...

What prospects *__like__* from salespeople...
- Only pertinent facts that describe the benefits of your products or services...solutions to problems
- The truth

- No bashing of the competition
- Testimonials to back up claims
- The opportunity to contact customers who do business with you
- Appreciation for their business
- Follow up

What prospects ***do not like*** to hear from salespeople...
- A tremendous amount of information -- "information overload"
- How you took advantage of their competition
- How badly you want their business
- How they can receive a better deal from you than from anyone else
- Over-promising and under-delivering
- Making excuses
- High-pressure sales tactics

Remember, the basic rule is that it is generally five times easier to sell to your present or past customers than it is to find a new customer. The reason is that you have already developed a relationship with your customer and as a good salesperson you need to leverage the relationship to see how you can more effectively serve your customer's needs. Many salespeople leave money on the table because they do not practice the principles of cross-selling and up selling.

By cross-selling we mean creating a sales process for you to sell new products and services to your current customers. For example, through suggestive selling techniques you can offer additional products and/or services that a customer can purchase from you. Your customer may only be buying one product or service group from you, but if you present other product groups to them, along with how they might benefit the customer's business, they may want to buy those also. Perhaps they are even buying those products or services from another company and didn't realize you also sell them.

Too many salespeople assume the customers know all the products and services that you represent when actually they don't. Spend a little more time with each of your customers and explore ways that your other products or services might help them. The result will be higher sales from each of your customers.

Up selling means the ability to increase the total sales amount from each customer. Instead of buying 1,000 units of a product, give them a good reason, such as a quantity discount, to buy 2,000 units. You can actually double your sales and your commissions this way. However, you need to give your customer solid reasons to purchase larger quantities from you which are usually based upon various pricing models. These pricing models can be divided into quantity discounts or annual discount programs.

A quantity discount means that if they order more at the time of purchase, they will receive a discount. An annual discount program will give your customer a discount based upon purchases made over a 12-month period. The advantage of this is that they save money and you have your customer's guaranteed business annually, keeping the competition away.

By using the cross-selling or up selling techniques you can drive higher volume through your most valuable asset—your current customers.

Important *Relationship Building Principles* you should know…

- The number one reason why businesses will lose customers is not because of inferior quality, prices, or lack of service selections, but because of an *attitude of indifference* shown by the employee or the employer of that company. In fact, 68% of all lost business is because of this attitude of indifference that is felt by the customer.
- It is generally *five times more costly* to create a new customer than it is to keep a present customer.

- A very good thought that summarizes these principles is "business goes where it's invited but it stays where it's truly appreciated."
- The American Management Association says that an estimated *55% of future business* comes from your present customers.
- The average business will *lose approximately 20% of its customers each year* for various reasons.
- Effective customer service departments within companies or the management should solicit customer feedback which allows problems to be solved. You can *win back as many as 74%* of dissatisfied customers with this technique.
- According to a recent study for every one complainer or dissatisfied customer, there are 26 who feel like complaining but who do not...they just take their business somewhere else.
- The 3/11 rule states that if you have a good experience with a business you will tell three other people; if you have a bad experience with a business you will tell 11 other people.

Practice building solid relationships and you will generate many repeat sales, fueling your career in sales as well.

Chapter
13

HUMOR

Good humor will break down a lot of sales resistance

To make your sales presentations more enjoyable for your prospects, use humor when appropriate. Making your prospect laugh is truly a good icebreaker. All people like to laugh. Your prospects are no different. Some sales presentations can be perceived as stressful and somewhat boring so try to create a more enjoyable experience. Studies show that humor can make you more persuasive because humor mentally disarms people. It allows them to take down their guard and to become more fully engaged with your presentation and conversations with you and more open to your suggestions.

Here are some key benefits that you will gain in using humor in your presentations...

- **Relaxed mood** – by providing humor you have a greater opportunity to make your prospects relax. When they are relaxed they can be more open to what you are saying versus being resistant toward what you are presenting

- **Increases confidence** – by using humor in your presentation, you are perceived as a more engaging and confident sales professional
- **Touching the heart** – humor touches the heart more effectively than facts, data, and information-dumping...and we know one of the principal methods that people use when buying is emotionally based
- **Building a bond** – when you have a sense of humor you create better rapport and more effectively connect or build a better bond with your prospect. When you are both laughing, you have something in common and this bond is created that enhances communication which helps build a good relationship and can lead to a new sale.

As you develop an element of humor in your sales presentations you will see that it becomes one of the key methods of selling to the heart...how most sales are really won.

Chapter
14

OBJECTIONS

Sales objections are good...you just need the ability
to overcome them

No one said that a career in sales was going to be easy. Unlike other positions, you encounter constant rejection and resistance, as well as objections to your presentations and your products and services. These objections can wear you out and have a tendency to diminish your motivation. But here's the good news...successful sales presentations contain approximately 50% more objections that non-successful sales presentations...and you just have to overcome the sales objections to win the sale. Compare the prospect who gives you sales objections to the one who is quiet and reserved and really doesn't say much at all. The person who gives sales objections is interested but you have to overcome the objections to go to the next level. The prospects who are not interested are usually very apathetic and give you little information to use as a stepping stone to getting a yes.

To win the emotional and the rational sales you have to practice some key characteristics in your presentation, including...

- **Have a positive attitude** – you need to maintain a positive attitude and listen to the objections of the prospect without becoming defensive or argumentative
- **Anticipate** – you should know some of the key objections you are going to hear; anticipate them along with some possible solutions and be prepared to overcome those objections
- **Repeat the objection**—you should always repeat the objection to clarify that you heard the prospect correctly and understand their objection; also lets the prospect know that you are truly listening to what they are saying
- **Distinguish between an objection and an excuse**—the objection is a legitimate concern about your company's products or services that you need to overcome; an excuse, on the other hand, is just a reason to get rid of you

Many times a prospect will tell you "no" but that means "not right now," not necessarily sometime in the future. Times change, decision makers change, competitors change, etc. so when you do accept a "no" as a temporary answer, be sure to call back at a reasonable time in the future and you may be able to change that "no" to a "yes."

You may also be able to change a "no" to a "yes" by

providing additional information. Some buyers really do not know why they are saying "no" so by providing additional information, you may overcome their objections. Keep providing additional benefits and reasons why your company represents a good decision for them. Remember, a sale often begins after the customer says "no."

An effective way to overcome objections and get the real objection clarified is to use the "suppose" tactic. This technique works because it eliminates one critical element that may be blocking the entire reason for the prospect not doing business with you. Here are three examples of using the suppose technique...

- *Ms. Prospect, Suppose that condition didn't exist. Could we then have the option to do business with you?*
- *Mr. Prospect, Suppose we could prove to you that we could fill this need for your company. Could we then have the opportunity to do business with you?*
- *Mr. Prospect, Suppose we can adjust our pricing to meet your budget requirements. Could we then have the opportunity to have you as a customer?*

Of course, you are going to encounter the difficult buyer. These people seem to be in the "doom and gloom" state no matter what you say or do and there seems to be little reaction to your presentation. In that case there is an effective question you can use...

- *Mr. Prospect, Can you please tell me what the reasons are that are in the way of us doing business together?*

This question reverses the process and puts the burden on your prospect to explain why. Based upon the answer, you will be able to determine two things...

- The real reasons why you are not getting the business so that you can truly try to overcome the hard-core objections

OR

- You will be able to determine if the buyer has legitimate objections or is merely making excuses why he does not want to do business with your company

It's important to understand this because real objections can be overcome. Excuses, on the other hand, are difficult to overcome because many times they are based on a prejudice or bias that the buyer may have.

The top three sales objections and how to overcome them are...

- *"We are happy with our current supplier"*

  I am pleased that you are happy with your current supplier. You obviously have made a good choice. However I'd like to point out a few ways that our company is different and how we could be of additional help to you and your company. (you would then list two or three benefits that make your company different from their current vendor for reasons that may benefit their buying from you, in addition to their current supplier)

- *"Your prices are too high"*

  I'm sure your company wants the best price and the best value...isn't that true?

  Prospect says "yes" and then you would talk about the value and benefits that your company offers. You have changed control of the discussion by taking the focus off the lowest price to offering the best value. Remember, most companies are looking for the best value versus the lowest price.

- *"We don't have a need for your company's products or services right now"*

  I can really appreciate the timing in your decision-making process. Could you please tell me when your company will be making a decision about products or services like ours?

71

The prospect will then give you a date or general time of year and you can then ask permission to contact them 1-3 months before that date.

The second method to overcome this objection is to offer an option to purchase your product or service on a smaller scale at a lower price or on a trial basis in order to initiate some immediate action. Often this trial program will lead to larger sales.

The average prospect is sometimes programmed to give you an objection just to get rid of you but many times these objections are not valid. Professional salespeople will stay in the game, which is necessary to eventually win the sale. Persistence is the key.

Chapter
15

PASSION

*Passions, great passions, can elevate the soul
to do great things*

When you sell with passion, you sell with excitement and energy, creating more emotional connections with your prospect. Enthusiasm is about excitement in yourself, your products and services, your prospect and his company, and about life in general. Your natural passion and enthusiasm are contagious and will increase your persuasive influence. Someone once said, *"Nothing happens that is great without true enthusiasm and passion."* Through passion and joy you can accomplish more than twice the work you can normally do without passion. Your energy will increase when you are selling if it's fueled by passion. Passion is that important competitive edge that is one of the main ingredients for all success in this life.

Passion is about conveying positive feelings to your prospects. It's not about all the product knowledge you have, but it's really about how you feel and getting the prospect to feel the same way about what you are selling. When this enthusiastic feeling is communicated the chance for winning a new sale increases significantly. The belief that you have in yourself and your company and your products and services is what creates the enthusiasm that you need to have as a winning salesperson.

Here is a great research study about passion and doing what you love: In a study of 1,500 college business students it was found that 1,245 were primarily looking to make a lot of money as a result of their Business degree. The other 255 students deeply cared about what they were doing and what they were learning. Many years later researchers went back and found that the highest income earners, including millionaires, came from the 255 students—with the exception of one person. As they say, *"Do what you love and the money will follow."*

The happiest and most successful salespeople really don't go to "work" because of the passion they have for themselves, their sales career, and for the life they have. Research shows that every single dose of affirmative emotion, such as excitement, enthusiasm, and caring, produces positive changes in your brainwaves which accentuate your passion. True passion equals your continued success.

It's good to be excited about yourself in your life. The best way to do this is to concentrate on the good things that you have and don't think about what you don't have. Adopt an *attitude of gratitude* by being truly optimistic about yourself and your future. After all, you only have one life to live, so why not live it to the fullest extent and focus on all the blessings you have. You are unique, so be thankful for your unique qualities and make the most of them. When you do this your enthusiasm will continue to increase, making you a more effective salesperson.

Secondly, you should be interested in what you are doing. The greater love you have for what you are doing, the greater amount of enthusiasm you will project. The key here is to become truly involved with what you are selling. You can generate more interest in what you are doing by becoming more knowledgeable about the industry in which you are selling. For example, if you are selling for an Internet marketing firm, become an expert in the Internet and knowledgeable of the basic concepts of marketing. By increasing your knowledge of the general industry and more specifically, the company you are presenting to, your enthusiasm will increase and you may even be viewed as a subject matter expert in that field. You become a trusted advisor.

All great salespeople and leaders possess an element of enthusiasm and passion in their sales presentations. Remember, *"Knowledge gets you into the game, but passion usually wins it."*

CONFIDENCE

Destroy fear and your confidence will soar

A sales manager of a major company who hired and trained thousands of salespeople was once asked what really separates the outstanding salespeople from the mediocre ones. He simply said it was their level of self-confidence. A salesperson might know everything about their product or service but they may not appear to be a truly confident salesperson.

Product knowledge is absolutely necessary for you to become a high achieving salesperson, but you need to be much more than a walking encyclopedia of information to project confidence to your prospects. So what are some of the other ways to develop a strong sense of self-confidence in yourself and your company? Here are some helpful tips...

* **Destroy Fear** – fear is one of the greatest obstacles to creating self-confidence. The salesperson could be thinking what if I don't reach my quota this month? What if I don't make enough money this year? What if I get fired—how will I be able to find another job—maybe I'll become homeless.

- All of these negative thoughts created by fear zap a person's confidence. Most fear is self-induced which creates mental monsters in your head...worry, tension, embarrassment, panic...all come from repetitive negative thinking. When this negative energy occupies a person's mind, it greatly hinders a person's success and productivity.

You can conquer fear by using a two-step method. First, isolate and clarify your fear. Determine exactly what you are afraid of and be as specific as possible. Second, develop a plan of action to conquer your fear. For example, if you are afraid of not being able to reach your sales quota and maybe getting fired, develop a plan of action that you will make four more sales calls a day—20 more per week—which should prevent losing your job. In other words, you are taking a positive step to reduce your fear.

- **Positive Thoughts** – when you wake up each morning and throughout the day feed your mind with small continuous positive thoughts. Remember, the majority of people are programmed to think negative thoughts. In fact, psychologists say that about 80% of thoughts are negative. So the key here is to think about positive things...turn your mind into a positive thought factory...and it will increase your personal self-confidence and productivity.

- **Visualize** – many successful people use the technique of visualization. They repeat over and over in their minds and visualize success before it actually happens. For example, you may be competing for a major account and you could use this technique to visualize winning the account, signing the agreement, and receiving your large commission check and being congratulated by your boss for a job well done. Visualizing will help you actually create the steps to make this all happen.

- **Be Creative** – you can increase your self-confidence in sales by not acting like a salesperson, but as a consultant, by providing good creative ideas. If you can offer new ideas to your prospect rather than just trying to sell them something, your value to your prospect will increase. They will respect you more and your self-confidence will naturally increase.

- **Industry Expert** – besides just having good product knowledge about what you sell, become an expert in the industry. For example, you may be selling software to the manufacturing marketplace. You become knowledgeable about your specific software—both features and benefits—but go the extra mile and find out more about manufacturing as a general industry. Your confidence will increase because you can talk intelligently about manufacturing as an industry, including current conditions and future trends, especially as they apply to the businesses you are calling on. By spending time reading industry articles in industry publications and on the internet you will increase your knowledge. Then you will be perceived as more of an expert or consultant than just an average salesperson.

- **Testimonials** – seek out customer testimonials about success they have had with you, your company, and your products/services. Put these letters in a nice folder and use this in your presentations. This will increase their confidence in you and your company. Testimonials truly work so be sure to use them.

- **Rejection** – every salesperson receives more no's than yeses. In fact, a .300 hitter in baseball (very good average) actually means they fail 7 of 10 times to get a hit and still make $10 million+ per year. Build a strong wall between you and your feelings of rejection and your ability to be a top-performing sales professional will increase. Do not take rejection in a personal way but cement in your mind that it is a "Numbers Game" and you will eventually win as long as you are persistent in your efforts and keep making sales calls. Your persistence in overcoming rejection will increase your confidence significantly and vice versa.

- **Read** – discipline yourself to read at least one hour per day, concentrating on inspirational and motivational books. Some great selections include:

o   *Think & Grow Rich* by Napoleon Hill
o   *The Magic of Thinking Big* by David Schwartz
o   *See You at the Top* by Zig Ziglar
o   *How to Win Friends & Influence People* by Dale Carnegie

Through a planned system of reading you will become more knowledgeable and motivated as a true sales leader. Reading consistently is like putting money in the bank.

Chapter
17

OPTIMISM

Optimistic salespeople always sell more

In many studies it was found that optimistic salespeople sell more than salespeople who are pessimistic. When an optimistic person makes a sales call they really believe they're going to get a sale before they even meet the prospect. They're optimistic about getting the results they really want...a new sale. In addition, studies indicate that optimistic people generally live longer, have higher incomes, longer and better marriages, and have much better health resulting in fewer strokes and heart attacks.

Happiness and optimism are contagious so create happy prospects through your optimism and they will be more likely to buy from you. When you make a sales call you are really calling on three different types of buyers:

- **The cynical, negative buyer**—this type of buyer has a basic distrust of all salespeople, possibly because of previous experiences. This will be a challenge for you but it is very possible to change this person's perception of salespeople by your strong optimism in yourself, your company and the solutions you are offering.

- **The indifferent buyer**—this type of buyer seems to lack energy and interest in you or your company. Your optimism can change this person's indifference to interest in what you are presenting. Again, optimism is contagious
- **The happy buyer**—this buyer really wants to be helped, which, of course, is the easiest type of person to sell to. Your optimism will generate a natural bond with this person making it much easier to win a sale.

Here are some tips to become a more optimistic person in your sales career...

- **Adversity** – everyone faces adversity in life, especially in sales, but the key is not that you face adversity, it's how you deal with it that's important. It is not how many times you get hit in this life, it's about how many times you actually get up. When you face a sales situation that is filled with rejection and bad news it can really affect you. You need to take control by creating positive action—by calling on a new prospect as soon as possible because you are looking for a positive event or even a new sale to eliminate the adversity you encountered previously. Search for new experiences that are good and that will increase your motivation to keep you moving in a positive manner. You will become more optimistic.

- **Associates and Friends** – another study indicates that most people average five or six close associates or friends. Pessimistic people are attracted to pessimistic people because these people drown in a pool of self-pity and misery loves company. On the other hand, optimistic people always look for the good and will not be hindered by the bad economy, a recession, economic hard times, etc. A pessimistic person will say that no one is buying and an optimistic person will say someone is buying...I just have to work harder to find them. Choose your associates and friends from the optimistic ones and stay away from the doom and gloom people you may know.

- **Short term** – optimistic people realize that adversity is usually just temporary...you may have lost a battle but your goal is to keep your thinking and actions on winning the war. If you experienced some unexpected setbacks, come up with some new ways and ideas, such as visiting with your current customers who may generate new sales for you. In addition, spend one to two hours a night reading books that promote positive thinking, such as *Think and Grow Rich* by Napoleon Hill or *How To Stop Worrying and Start Living* by Dale Carnegie.

- **Think Results** – as an optimistic salesperson you

should think in results, not defeats. Keep the end in sight and you really need to focus on sales results and not get bogged down by all the excuses and small hurdles you must get over in order to be successful. Pessimistic people wish the good old days would come back with their greener pastures. Optimistic people go out and create those greener pastures.

Here are some additional tips that you can use to increase the attitude of optimism in your sales career...

- Concentrate on the good things you have to be thankful for—your health, your family, your job. Optimistic thoughts create positive energy which drives a sense of accomplishment.

- Every morning when you wake up, practice PMP (Positive Mental Programming) by repeating positive affirmations, such as "Today is going to be a great day! Today is going to be a great day!" In a way, you can say this is brainwashing yourself—but it works! Try it!

- And, there is one additional quote which is very reflective about having enthusiasm and optimism, "We act in this life as though we need furs, jewels, money, fancy cars, etc. to be happy...when all we really need is something to be enthusiastic about."

- Optimism is energy which constantly nourishes the mind and soul to overcome many of the roadblocks we encounter in sales...to give us the endurance to ultimately win!

Optimism is a choice you make each day...when you wake up you have the choice to put on your optimistic "glasses"—not your pessimistic ones. If you practice each and every day becoming more optimistic in your thinking, two things will happen. First, you become a happier person and second, your sales will also increase. Optimism is a very strong catalyst for your continued sales success and your happiness in life as well...it's all up to you.

Chapter
18

APPRECIATION

*The two most important words in the English
language are "Thank You"*

On a bulletin board in a florist shop there was a quote that said, *"the two most important words in the English language are Thank You."* It's fairly obvious that the florist wanted you to buy more flowers to say thank you as well as sending flowers on other occasions. As a sales professional, it is not practical to send flowers to every prospect you visit but you can show sincere appreciation for meeting with you and most importantly, for their business when they become a new client of yours.

Studies indicate that one of the most important needs that all people have is to feel needed, wanted, and appreciated. Feeling appreciated generally gives a person a certain glow (a feeling of value—that they really count). Remember, *"Business goes where it's invited and stays where it's appreciated."* Make sure your customers know that you appreciate their business. Develop a personalized appreciation program to show how much you value your customers' business. Your program could include some of these ideas...

- **Thank you notes** – Write a personal note thanking every prospect for their time and consideration…and, of course, every customer for their business. Most people agree that a personal, handwritten thank you note will have a greater impact on the prospect than a standard email thank you. Handwritten thank you notes are more personable and communicate a softer touch to a customer than a simple email might. Handwritten notes touch the heart.

- **Lunches** – a good sign of showing appreciation could be taking your customers to lunch. This would be well received by most customers. With lunches there are fewer interruptions and you can have a more relaxed environment to talk with them.

- **Holiday Gifts** – send customers a small, but appropriate thank you gift at the holiday season toward the end of the year. By showing an attitude of gratitude, you will develop strong and lasting relationships.

CHARISMA

Charisma is a powerful magnet for attracting new customers

Having charisma, as a salesperson, means that you have a personality that attracts people to you. Charismatic people radiate joy, passion, enthusiasm and optimism—all the things we have discussed—leading to increased persuasion in your sales process. As a charismatic sales professional you will also instill a greater level of trust, one of the basic foundations to winning and keeping customers.

Mastering the 'art of the sale' is having the 3 C's— Confidence, Conviction, and Charisma. Let's discuss each one.

- When you display *confidence* you are more convincing. People are inclined to listen to you, people are more inclined to believe in you and your company. In addition, your confidence creates an image of authority and of being a knowledgeable expert leading to a commitment.

- When you have *conviction* as a salesperson you have belief in yourself and your company's products or services. A strong sense of conviction will give you the power to overcome the rejections that you encounter in some of your sales calls. As you have experienced, there have been disappointments, setbacks, and sales that you thought you were going to get but they fell through. Having conviction is a strong ingredient to overcome these setbacks and to keep moving in a positive manner toward your next sale.

- As a *charismatic* salesperson you will be unique and remembered in relationship to your sales competitors who have no spark, no energy, and little passion for what they are selling. Your charisma will set you apart from the companies with whom you are competing. Charisma is another powerful element that helps you to sell to the heart to win new customers.

Here are some suggestions to become more charismatic in your sales presentations. Have fun...enjoy what you are doing...smile...be happy...inject some humor in your presentations. Be inspiring about your products and services and be knowledgeable about your industry. Be confident by providing new information to help your prospects. Be conversational in your presentations and don't lecture. Concentrate on what you can give and what you can share to help them, not what you can take. Look professional...your appearance will help build a positive image in the prospect's mind. If you look good, they may think you must also do good work. Be thankful … show respect and appreciation for the prospect's time and attention and don't take anything for granted. And, above all, your charisma will be enhanced by your honesty. If you don't know something, admit it and then get back to your customer with the correct information. Never exaggerate or over-promise. Be sincere, well-mannered and completely fair and honest in all of your conversations with your prospects and your customers.

Your charismatic personality will be a magnet for attracting and keeping many new customers, as well as keeping the customers that you have.

Chapter
20

W.I.F.M.

*Most people are motivated by their own
self-interests, not yours...they think
What's In It For Me*

When selling to the "heart" you discover and push the right buttons...then answer their question "What's In It For Me" (W.I.I.F.M.).

Simply put, people will buy from you based upon what they will get...what they will gain from your products or services. They will not buy from you because they want to help you reach your sales goals, but they will buy from you if they believe that their purchase can help them in their business.

In order to properly find the answer to W.I.I.F.M. you need to ask questions to determine the real needs and wants of your prospects. This is one of the major weaknesses of many sales presentations—the salesperson simply does not ask enough questions to find out what the prospect really needs or wants. You cannot assume anything when you are selling. Their current situation does not necessarily provide keys to the sale. For example, it would be a mistake to think that a prospect would only buy from you if you have the lowest price. Their needs may exceed buying the lowest price in the products and services that you represent. For example, perhaps they purchased the lowest price previously and did not have a good experience. The real need may be for a company that offers superior service or consistent delivery systems, such as yours.

In his classic book, *How to Win Friends and Influence People,* Dale Carnegie states that one of the key principles in sales and in life is to show interest in the other person and to get them to talk about themselves. When you show interest in another person by asking questions about them and listening with interest to their answers, an amazing thing happens. They will like you. This is the same principle that applies to W.I.I.F.M. People are motivated by their own self-interest. Most people are highly focused on themselves which represents a very good opportunity for you to become a star in your selling process if you focus on the principle of W.I.I.F.M. and give them what they want...not what you want.

Unfortunately, many salespeople are too focused on closing the sale and making the commission, not focused on the best interest of their prospects. This is a major issue of many salespeople when trying to close sales. It's not about closing the sale; it's about providing the needs and wants of your prospects. When you can satisfy these important needs through your company's products and services, they will buy from you. You have created the right opportunity for them to buy from you. Sales is not a hard-closing process; it's a process whereby you find the key to answer the prospect's question of W.I.I.F.M. You are selling to their heart and they are buying from their heart because they feel you can help them based upon what they both want and need.

THE HALO EFFECT

*Your "halo" will generate new referrals
and customers*

The halo effect occurs when you have done a great job for one company and you tell your prospect about it because it means you can do a great job for their company as well. In other words, your "halo" touches other people to create a good impression that you can also provide similar results for them. People are programmed to associate one good thing with another...and, in the same sense, they associate one bad thing with another. Become a sales "angel" with a bright halo to attract and keep customers.

Actually, you may have developed a good reputation by providing excellent service and products to your current customers. These relationships can create referrals that can lead to new customers. You would probably agree that some of your best new customers have come from referrals from your current customers.

Referrals may come to you, but you also have to ask for them. Develop the habit of asking for referrals especially if your current customer is happy with your company, happy with you, and has been a consistent customer for many years.

There are certain specific referral techniques that you can use to generate a consistent flow of new potential customers. The correct way to ask for a referral would be to ask an open-ended question versus closed-ended question. For example, you would say, *"Bob, we really appreciate your business and you have been a good customer. Who do you know that I could call on and be able to use your name as a referral?"* Now Bob has to think of a few names to give you because Bob likes you and wants to help you.

The ineffective way to ask would be to say, *"Bob, do you know of anyone that I could call and use your name as a referral?"* The problem with this question is that it is too easy for Bob to say "no" because you have not given him the opportunity to think and go to work for you with some names. Many people are conditioned to say "no" without even thinking.

When you have developed a good "halo" with your current customers, make sure that halo touches other businesses who can become new customers for you.

T.E.A.M.

There is no "I" in the word TEAM

A good explanation of T.E.A.M. is Together Everyone Achieves More. In most cases, your sales calls are performed by you without any involvement from other people. However, teams can accomplish more than a single individual. Let us use a law of physics to illustrate this point. One horse can pull 4 tons of concrete; but 2 horses working side by side can actually pull 22 tons of concrete. Two horses working together can actually create over ten times more productivity. In the same sense, teams can accomplish a great deal more when working together for the same purpose

As a professional salesperson how can you use a team effort to increase your sales? Here are four ideas...

* **Sales manager** – if you have a sales manager, ask him or her to make a number of joint sales calls with you and ask for suggestions on how you can improve your sales presentations. In addition, you may be getting a number of sales objections that may be difficult to overcome. Your sales manager, because of his or her experience, may be able to teach you how

to overcome a number of these objections. An effective Sales Manager can become a great team member, offering fresh ideas and good sales tips that you can use on all of your sales calls.

- **Subject matter expert** – if you are involved in technical sales, a subject matter expert can become an important contributor to help you win new accounts. Everyone has their strengths and weaknesses. As a salesperson your strength can be building relationships but not necessarily being able to wrap your arms around complex technical information. In this case you could even invite a technician or a sales engineer to make specific sales calls with you to explain the technical aspects...again, working as a team.

- **Sales associate** – there are usually a number of salespeople in your company with defined territories and specific market segments or product knowledge. Perhaps there is a salesperson or associate in your company who is developing a good track record in selling to a specific market segment, such as manufacturing. This person could add additional firepower to your sales call by describing various success stories that helped them win a new customer in that industry. You and this sales associate would function as an effective team.

- **Sales support** – effective sales support is an important part of your sales team and your ability to win new accounts. Your sales support team may consist of administrators, proposal writers, and lead generators. All of these people can be very important in helping you achieve your sales goals. Try not to take your sales support team for granted. Everyone wants to feel needed and wanted and appreciated. Ask your sales support team out to lunch and show your appreciation for the good job they do for you by helping you with your sales efforts and achievement. Always share the glory.

Concentrate on building and becoming part of the sales team and you will be rewarded because a team can accomplish much more than a single person…and, remember, there is no "I" in the word "TEAM."

Chapter
23

CREATIVITY

*One new creative idea can result in a
new customer*

One of the best ways to connect emotionally with your prospect is to provide creative ideas and solutions. Instead of just "information dumping" and reciting a canned sales presentation, become a creative thinker for your prospect. When you do this you will be unique among your competitors and often come away with more sales.

As we discussed before, every sale is really a solution to a problem. In order to solve problems you need to focus on creative thinking. In many companies new ways of doing a more effective way of selling their products and services and improving profits are right in front of them. However, these people simply do not see them. They continue repeating the same processes and expect better results…which rarely happen.

As a professional salesperson you are unique because you bring a pair of fresh eyes that can provide new solutions and innovations. You can act as a source of new methods and ideas that maybe you learned from a similar business. You can transform yourself into a creative consultant versus just a normal salesperson trying to sell something.

In order to become more creative you have to believe that you are more creative than you might think. When the topic of creativity comes up in various discussions people say, *"Oh, I'm not really creative."* In most cases, they're relating creativity to some form of artistic skill, musical skill, etc. that they may not have. But creativity is a lot more than being a good artist, musician or writer. In fact, a sales career often offers many opportunities to be more creative than other professions.

Here are some ideas that you can use in your daily sales calls to become a creative resource rather than just an average salesperson…

- **Reduce negative thinking** – most of us are conditioned to negative thinking which, among many of the other things we've talked about, curtails our ability to think in a creative manner Here are some phrases/thoughts you should eliminate from your thinking and your sales process…
    o *"That's not practical"*
    o *"I've never done it that way before"*
    o *"It's not logical"*
    o *"I tried that before"*
    o *"It's too much work"*

- o   *"I don't have the time"*
- o   *"I don't have the money"*
- o   *"I don't think it will work"*

- **Ask the right questions** – your new creative powers are linked to your ability to ask the right questions. A management consultant once said, *"it takes a logical mind to spot the wrong answers, but it takes a creative mind to notice the wrong questions."* If you ask your prospect the wrong question, you will get the wrong answer which just leads back to the "normal" methods of doing business. No problems are solved because no creative results occurred. You must challenge the status quo of how your prospects make buying decisions and provide new creative ideas to them by asking the "right questions."

- **Be a sponge** – with your listening skills you must absorb…like a sponge…the answers the prospect is giving you about his needs and any problems he is having. Then as a sales professional, you need to come up with new ideas for your prospect. If the products or services you sell were successful for another of your customers, describe how they were effective and create a link to your prospect's situation that can help them achieve similar results. Think about all the knowledge you have absorbed and what you have achieved through your sales calls and realize that you can become a valuable creative resource for new solutions and ideas to help new customers and drive more sales.

- **Connect the "Unconnected"** – draw lines between different services or products that you are offering in order to develop a new value-added service or product for your prospect

- **Bundle** – group or bundle various products or services to provide a *total sales solution* that can make you and your company unique and more valuable in the prospect's mind

In summary, most of your prospects need new solutions and creative ideas to improve their business. You can be a creative power source to make this happen. Be creative and you will sell more now and well into the future.

Chapter

24

WIN-WIN

When you win for your customer,
you will win for yourself

When you make a sales call on a prospect you're not "out to get them" or trying to do something to them. On the contrary, your goal is to create a feeling of trust that can help them win in their business and when they win, then you win also. Many sales calls are made in the U.S. today with the salesperson's primary goal being to make a new sale to increase their commissions, often without consideration of whether what they are selling is appropriate for the prospect or not.

In Stephen Covey's book, *The 7 Habits of Highly Effective People*, one of the habits is to think "win-win." Mr. Covey describes win-win as a cooperative arena not a competitive one. He says win-win is a frame of mind which seeks mutual benefit in all human interactions and selling is definitely a human interaction.

Mr. Covey says that a person who projects a win-win attitude has three characteristics that are based on our ability to project specific feelings or emotions in our selling process. These key emotions are integrity, maturity, and a sense of sharing...when working with your prospects.

Integrity means sticking with your true feelings, values, and commitments. As we discussed before, many sales are lost because a salesperson failed to communicate trust. When you do not project integrity and fail to communicate good values, you will never sell anything— no matter how low the price is or how good the benefits are. You truly have to sell to a person's heart first and their head second. When you make a commitment to a prospect or customer you need to keep that commitment. It may be a very small commitment, such as returning a phone call at a certain time, but it is quite important that you keep that commitment because you are establishing an image of professionalism and trust in the prospect's mind. Most people buy from a state of mind usually driven by key emotional triggers and logical solutions.

Maturity is the second characteristic that you should have to create a win-win situation in your selling process. By this we mean expressing your ideas with courage and consideration for the feelings of others. Another way of describing this characteristic is specific use of empathy in dealing with your prospects and customers. Empathy is derived from a Greek word meaning pain. Great salespeople project empathy which is the natural ability to feel and really understand the prospect's situation—to feel their "pain". When a salesperson demonstrates this type of empathy, it helps to develop trust and the quality of communication and persuasion increases.

Practicing an attitude of sharing is the third characteristic of having a win-win environment which means there's plenty for everyone. Another way of describing this characteristic is to not be greedy in your sales process. Some salespeople make the mistake of trying to go for the "home run" in every sale, which is usually driven by wanting to achieve higher commissions by making a larger sale. The largest sales and accounts are very profitable but maybe it's better to take "baby steps" by trying to win a smaller sale and developing a good relationship with your new client, which you can then build into future and perhaps, even larger sales.

If you develop an attitude of win-win on each sales call, your sales will increase because you will be perceived, not as a pushy salesperson, but as a person who is driven by a win-win attitude for both your prospect/customer and for yourself. Everyone wins!!

GIVING BACK

*We make a living by what we get; we make
a life by what we give*

Giving back in this life is one of the key components of creating self-fulfillment and happiness. James M. Barrie, author of *Peter Pan*, said *"Those who bring sunshine to the lives of others cannot keep it from themselves."* It often seems to be true that you will be paid in one way or another for giving more service than is actually expected.

In order to develop more fulfillment and optimism in your life and your sales career become more involved in organizations, associations, ministries, charities, and your church. Then volunteer and get involved in events and activities whereby you can give back both your time and talents. Through this involvement you will find situations where you generally can help others who are perhaps less fortunate than you. Many times in life the act of giving is more important than receiving.

There is another benefit to becoming involved in organizations where you are giving back. That benefit is that you will meet many good people along the way who could potentially lead you to new business contacts or opportunities for your sales career. Networking is a proven method of meeting new and interesting people who lead to new future opportunities.

Through giving back you will be helping people who need your talents and energy. You will also meet new people whereby you could create some lasting friendships. You cannot lose.

Giving back can best be described as taking focus off of you and putting it on other people and their causes which are really bigger than you. True happiness is not about self—it's about giving to help others. Money doesn't bring happiness.

A survey was conducted some time ago where they compared the "happiness index" of six millionaires and six quadriplegics and the six quadriplegics really had a happier index than the six millionaires. How could this be? Well, the six people who had these disabilities were not focused on power and money, but perhaps on the more spiritual aspects of life and were not consumed by greed or money.

Here are some ideas that you can implement to experience the thrill of giving back:

- Set a specific goal for what you would like to accomplish in your business or your career and then take a portion of that money and give it to a non-profit association. Make this promise to yourself and you will be on your way to giving back to your world.
- Use your special talents in business to help other people achieve their goals. You can accomplish this through your church, Junior Achievement, civic organizations, mentoring groups, or maybe even an organization that you would create.

Dennis Gaskill said, "To help yourself, help others. Whatever good you do travels in a circle and returns to you many times over. But remember, life is not about what you get...it's about what you give and become." You make a living by what you get...you make a life by what you give.

Chapter
26

INSPIRATIONS
Powerful inspirations create personal motivation

Selling is not easy. You encounter many objections, rejections, and many dead ends. To increase your motivation and drive to win, you need to keep yourself "mentally pumped up" and inspired.

A good way to do this is to practice some of the inspirations from these quotes written by some of the greatest leaders who have ever lived.

Continuous positive thoughts will increase your success as a true sales leader.

ACHIEVEMENT

"Only those who dare to fail greatly can ever achieve greatly."
Unknown
"Unless you try to do something beyond what you have already mastered, you will never grow."
Ralph Waldo Emerson
"Some men dream of worthy accomplishments, while others stay awake and do them."

Unknown
"All things are difficult before they are easy."

John Norley
"All great achievements require time."

Anne Frank

"I was taught very early that I would have to depend entirely upon myself; that my future lay in my own hands."

Darius O. Mills

"What the mind can conceive and believe, it can achieve."

Napoleon Hill

ATTITUDES

"People can alter their lives by altering their attitudes."

William James

"I cannot change yesterday. I can only make the most of today, and look with hope toward tomorrow."

Unknown

BELIEF

"To accomplish great things we must not only act, but also dream; not only plan, but also believe."

Unknown

"Work joyfully and peacefully, knowing that right thoughts and right efforts will inevitably bring about right results."

James Allen

"A will finds a way."

Orison S. Marden

"Nothing splendid has ever been achieved except by those who dared believe that something inside of them was superior to circumstance."

Bruce Barton

"They conquer who believe they can."

Latin Proverb

"The strongest single factor in prosperity is believing you can do it, believing you deserve it, believing you will get it."

Jerry Gillies

"In order to succeed, we must first believe that we can."

Michael Korda

A man is literally what he thinks."

James Allen

CONFIDENCE

"Confidence is half the victory."

Yiddish Proverb

COURAGE

"Courage is resistance to fear...mastery of fear...not absence of fear."

Mark Twain

"He who loses wealth loses much; he who loses a friend loses more; but he who loses courage loses all."

Cervantes

"One man with courage is a majority."

Andrew Johnson

"It takes courage to push yourself to places that you have never been...to test your limits...to break through barriers."

Unknown

DESIRE

"The kind of people I look for to fill top management spots are the mavericks. These are the guys who try to do more than they're expected to do – they always reach."

Lee Iacocca

'Do or do not; there is no try."

Yoda

"The intensity of your desire governs the power with which the force is directed."

John McDonald

"The starting point of all achievement is desire. Weak desires bring weak results, just as a small amount of fire makes a small amount of heat."

Napoleon Hill

"Desire creates the power."

Raymond Holliwell

"Desire sees the invisible, feels the intangible and achieves the impossible."

Unknown

119

DREAM

"Cherish your dreams. They are the children of your soul, the blueprints of your ultimate achievements."

Napoleon Hill

"Your dreams are an index to your greatness."

Unknown

"When you cease to dream you cease to live."

Malcolm S. Forbes

"The future belongs to those who believe in the beauty of their dreams."

Eleanor Roosevelt

"Those who have achieved great things have been dreamers."

Orison S. Marden

ENTHUSIASM

"We act as though comfort was the chief requirement of life when all we need to make us happy is something to be enthusiastic about."

Unknown

EXPECTATIONS

"It's a funny thing about life. If you refuse to accept anything but the best, you very often get it."

Somerset Maugham

"Life will always be to a large extent what we ourselves make it."

Samuel Smiles

FAILURE

"Failure is only the opportunity to more intelligently begin again."

Henry Ford

"Don't be afraid to fail. Learn from your failures and go on to the next challenge. It's OK. If you're not failing, you're not growing."

H. Stanley Judd

"Success is never final and failure is never fatal."

Unknown

"Act as though it were impossible to fail."

Unknown

FOCUS

"The secret of life is to know who you are and where you are going."

Unknown

"If you don't know where you are going, how can you expect to get there?"

Basil S. Walsh

"You may not have been responsible for your heritage, but you are responsible for your future."

Unknown

FUN

"People rarely succeed at anything unless they have fun doing it."

Unknown

GIVING

"When you cease to make a contribution you begin to die."

Eleanor Roosevelt

GOALS

"This one step – choosing a goal and sticking to it – changes everything."

Scott Reed

"A man without a purpose is like a ship without a rudder."

Thomas Carlyle

121

GREATNESS

"To endure is greater than to dare...to keep heart when all have lost it – who can say this is not greatness?"

William M. Thackeray

HAPPINESS

"Most people are about as happy as they make up their minds to be."

Abraham Lincoln

"Happiness is not a state to arrive at, but a manner of traveling."

Margaret Lee Runbeck

HEART

"To measure the man, measure his heart."

Malcolm S. Forbes

HOPE

"He who has health, has hope; and he who has hope, has everything."

Arabian Proverb

IDEAS

"A mind stretched by a new idea never regains its original dimensions."

Oliver Wendell Holmes

IMAGINATION

"We are told never to cross a bridge till we come to it, but this world is owned by men who have 'crossed bridges' in their imagination far ahead of the crowd."

Speakers Library

IMPROVEMENT

"Of all our human resources, the most precious is the desire to improve."

Unknown

"If there's a way to do it better...find it."

Thomas A. Edison

INSPIRATION

"Those who bring sunshine to the lives of others, cannot keep it from themselves."

James Barrie

INTEGRITY

"Your only obligation in any lifetime is to be true to yourself."

Richard Bach

LEADERSHIP

"Real leaders are ordinary people with extraordinary determination."

Unknown

"Leaders expect to win in advance. Life is a self-fulfilling prophecy."

Unknown

"Do not follow where the path may lead. Go instead where there is no path and leave a trail."

Unknown

"The speed of the leader determines the rate of the pack."

Unknown

"Give a man a fish and you feed him for a day. Teach a man to fish you feed him for a lifetime."

Chinese proverb

LUCK

"Be grateful for luck, but don't depend on it."

Unknown

OBSTACLES

"Because there are obstacles, the shortest line between two points is rarely straight."

Unknown

OPPORTUNITIES

"We are continually faced by great opportunities, brilliantly described as unsolvable problems."

Unknown

"Problems become opportunities when the right people come together."

Robert Redford

"Opportunity often comes in the form of misfortune or temporary defeat."

Napoleon Hill

"Each problem has hidden in it an opportunity so powerful that it literally dwarfs the problem."

Joseph Sugarman

"In the middle of difficulty lies opportunity."

Albert Einstein

"Most successful men have not achieved their distinction by having some new talent or opportunity presented to them. They have developed the opportunity that was at hand."

Bruce Barton

"The golden opportunity you are seeking is in yourself ... not in your environment ... not in luck or chance ... it is in yourself alone."

Orison Swett Marden

PERSEVERANCE

"I do not think there is any other quality so essential to success of any kind, as perseverance. It overcomes almost everything."

John D. Rockefeller

PERSISTENCE

"There is never a traffic jam on the extra mile."

Unknown

"Never, Never, Never Quit."

Winston Churchill

"Many of life's failures are men who did not realize how close they were to success when they gave up."

Unknown

"The majority of people meet with failure because of their lack of persistence in creating new plans to take the place of those which fail."

Napoleon Hill

"Most people give up just when they're about to achieve success. They quit on the one yard line. They give up at the last minute of the game, one foot from a winning touchdown."

H. Ross Perot

"Our greatest glory is not in never falling, but in rising every time we fall."

Confucius

"He conquers who endures."

Persius

"The rewards for those who persevere far exceed the pain that must precede the victory."

Ted Engstrom

"There is no education like adversity."

Benjamin Disraeli

PREPARATION

"Chance favors the prepared mind."

Louis Pasteur

SOLUTIONS

"Every problem has in it the seeds of its own solution."

Reinhold Niebuhr

SUCCESS

"The journey of a thousand miles starts with a single step."

Chinese proverb

"No one ever achieved worthwhile success who did not find themselves with at least one foot hanging well over the brink of failure."

Napoleon Hill

"Success is a journey, not a destination."

Ben Sweetland

"Success is simply a matter of luck. Ask any failure."

Unknown

"Whenever you see a successful business, someone once made a courageous decision."

Peter Daucher

"We make a living by what we get. But we make a life by what we give."

Unknown

"Success seems to be connected with action. Successful men keep moving. They make mistakes. But they don't quit."

Conrad Hilton

"He has achieved success who has lived well, laughed often, and loved much."

Unknown

"The road to success has many tempting parking places."

Steve Potter

"Success doesn't come to you ... you go to it."

Marva Collins

"The price of success is perseverance. The price of failure comes cheaper."

Unknown

"Each time you are honest and conduct yourself with honesty, a success force will drive you toward greater success."

Joseph Sugarman

"The successful person will profit from their mistakes and try again in a different way."

Dale Carnegie

"Always remember that your own resolution to succeed is more important than anything else."

Abraham Lincoln

"One man has enthusiasm for 30 minutes, another for 30 days, but the man who has it for 30 years makes a success of his life."

Edward B. Butler

"Not in time, place or circumstances, but in the person lies success."

Charles B. Rouss

"Success seems to be largely a matter of hanging on after others have let go."

William Feather

TALENTS

"Use the talents you possess, for the woods would be very silent if no birds sang except the best."

Unknown

TEAMWORK

"A candle loses none of its light by lighting another candle."

Unknown

THINKING

"Thinking is the essence of wisdom."

Persian proverb

"The best way to escape a problem is to solve it."

Anonymous

"Whether you think you can or think you can't – you are right."

Henry Ford

VALUE

"If you really do put a small value upon yourself, rest assured that the world will not raise the price."

Unknown

VICTORY

"Accept the challenges so that you may feel the exhilaration of victory."

General George S. Patton

"History has demonstrated that the most notable winners usually encountered heartbreaking obstacles before they triumphed."

B. C. Forbes

"Remember you will not always win. Some days, the most resourceful individual will taste defeat. But there is always tomorrow."

Maxwell Maltz

"All of the significant battles are waged within the self."

Sheldon Kopp

VISION

"Go as far as you can see, and when you get there, you will see farther."

Anonymous

"The only limits are, as always, those of vision."

James Broughton

"The empires of the future are empires of the mind."

Winston Churchill

"The entrepreneur is essentially a visualizer and an actualizer. He sees exactly how to make it happen."

Robert L. Schwartz

128

Made in the USA
Middletown, DE
19 August 2020